S0-BSK-550

ADRIFT!

ADRIFT!
Boating Safety for Children

Story by Joan Neudecker
Activities by Colleen Politano

Illustrated by Chris Buffett

Porthole Press Ltd.
Sidney, British Columbia
1986

**Copyright © 1986 by Colleen Politano
and Joan Neudecker**
Copyright Chris Buffett (drawings)
Edited by Michael Coney
Text set by The Typeworks,
Vancouver, B.C.
Printed in Canada
Published by Porthole Press Ltd.
2082 Neptune Road,
Sidney, B.C.   V8L 3X9

Canadian Cataloguing in Publication
Data:

Politano, Colleen, 1946–
    Adrift!

ISBN 0-919931-08-1

1. Survival (after airplane acidents,
shipwrecks, etc.). 2. Boats and
boating—
Safety measures. I. Neudecker, Joan,
1941–
II. Buffett, Chris III. Title.

GV777.6.P64
1986   613.6'9   C86-090080-0

All rights reserved. No part of this
publication may be reproduced, stored
in a retrieval system or transmitted, in
any form or by any means, electronic,
mechanical, photocopying, recording
or otherwise, without the prior
permission of the copyright owner.

Contents

*Practical hints and activities.

Acknowledgements

We could not have written *Adrift!* without the ideas and suggestions of friends and experts in the field of boating. Many activities from numerous sources have been adapted to suit our needs in trying to produce the most useful children's book on boating skills that we could offer. Special thanks from both of us go to Michael Coney, our mentor and publisher, for his encouragement, editing and expertise.

Introduction

The idea for *Adrift!* originated with an accident that could have been tragic, but fortunately had no long-lasting effects other than Joan Neudecker's desire to encourage other boaters to prepare themselves for an emergency or accident.

The Neudeckers had enjoyed at least thirteen years of boating before that eventful day. They had cruised and explored the area many times. However, perhaps because they were hungry and looking forward to lunch, they did not keep a good lookout as they sped towards their cruiser *Burman* in a ski-boat.

Their propeller struck a submerged deadhead, flipping the outboard motor up and into the bottom of the boat. The blades, still spinning, bit deeply into their son's ankle. They had no First Aid kit aboard, no blanket, no means of communication and no power. The wind was blowing them away from *Burman*, the rain was drizzling and the unwieldy hull responded only sluggishly to their paddling. Fortunately a fellow boater saw their predicament and they were rescued. They were lucky, and Joan and Lou knew it. Their main concern afterwards was to equip their children and their dinghy properly, and to encourage others to do the same.

Adrift! is written for children, but since no children should be in a dinghy without their parents' knowledge, it is also written for parents.

There are many books on the market about boating safety and seamanship which demand a considerable array of equipment and knowledge. These books are usually addressed to adults and, commendably, attempt to cover every conceivable situation. We, on the other hand, have adjusted our sights. By creating a story about two children adrift in a dinghy, we have concentrated on the essentials of that particular situation, and dealt with these essentials in a practical manner. The activities by Colleen provide practice and assist children to learn the concepts in an entertaining way. No equipment is used that could be dangerous, such as flares. The children use what is available in a creative manner. The equipment recommended in *Adrift!* is all essential.

We have aimed *Adrift!* at children between the ages of eight and twelve; younger children require supervision when using a dinghy. *Adrift!* is not intended as a self-teaching device; rather as an adventure story interspersed with activities that children can initiate themselves with limited guidance and supervision.

We have tried to be versatile in our presentation. *Adrift!* can be applied to any water situation: ocean, lake or river; and the skills learned will be of use aboard any small craft: dinghy, canoe or homemade boat.

Other CHILD SURVIVAL books are in preparation. Children should be taught to be resourceful and independent, and parents and teachers can do this by their own example and advice. A good book, however, can be a useful source of reminders and suggestions for preparing children to deal with everyday living in a practical manner. We hope that *Adrift!* meets this purpose.

1: Setting Off

"**W**e're off, Mom," said Karen as she pulled on the oars. The small white dinghy zig-zagged slightly till she got into the rhythm of rowing.

"Don't be gone too long," replied Mom, "and keep your lifejackets on."

The *Serendipity* seemed to become smaller and smaller as they got farther and farther away, until they couldn't see Mom anymore.

Roger put out his fishing line and leaned back to watch his rod bobbing gently up and down, while his sister rowed at a steady pace. He looked up at the sky. It was quite cloudy, in spite of the warm sun. He watched some crows on shore, arguing over something to eat. *Wouldn't it be wonderful to be able to fly*, he thought. He smiled at Sam, their dog, who was standing in the bow, sniffing the breeze and watching everything that moved. He wondered if Sam dreamed about flying, too. What a great dog! He was the best watchdog, the best hunter and the very best swimmer.

"Time to check your line, Roger," Karen suggested. "Quick, it's starting to jiggle really fast now. Reel it in!"

"I'm reeling, I'm reeling," replied Roger.

"Oh, it's stopped. Have you lost the fish?"

"Yes, I have," replied Roger indignantly, "and it's all your fault."

"Why is it my fault?"

"Because you stopped rowing and my line sank."

"Well, if that's the way you feel, let's go back. You row!"

"Okay, I'll row but let's not go back yet. Let's explore."

"Do up your lifejacket first. You know you're supposed to have it fastened."

They changed places carefully and Roger, not quite so smooth at rowing as his older sister, tried to keep the dinghy going where he wanted it to go. He watched his wake and tried to keep it straight. As he rowed, he pretended he was a prisoner on a pirate ship and Karen was the enemy captain. Sam looked like the figurehead as he stretched out as far as he could. Roger rowed closer to shore, watching a mother duck and her family of five ducklings swimming along.

"Look where you're going!" shouted the Captain. "Don't you see those rocks ahead?"

"Of course I see them. I just tried to see how close we could come without scraping the bottom," he answered, not wanting to admit that he had been daydreaming.

"You'll be sorry if you do scrape it. We won't be able to take the dinghy out again by ourselves."

"I'm hungry," Roger said, to change the subject.

"You're always hungry. I guess we could share one can of juice and one Granola bar. Then we'll still have another to share later. You're bound to get hungry again before we return to the *Serendipity*."

As they shared their snack, Roger shipped his oars and let the dinghy drift. They didn't notice that a wind was coming up and that it was pushing them away from the shore.

Suddenly Roger saw something in the water. Then it was gone. He stopped chewing and watched the spot where he had last seen it. It must have been his imagination. *Maybe it's a mermaid*, he thought, getting back into his pirate role once more. No! There it was again! It had a long pointed tail.

"What's that?" Karen had seen it too.

"Sh-h-h! You'll scare it away," Roger whispered, as a whiskery face with sharp brown eyes surfaced right beside the rowboat.

Sam stood like a statue, his nose twitching slightly and his tail straight out, in his best pointer style. It

became a staring game between Sam and the creature in the water.

"Let's follow it." Roger put the oars in place and began to row gently, like in the pirate days when they had to muffle their oars so that the enemy couldn't hear them coming.

They all sat as still as they could, never taking their eyes off the small, furry animal. Sometimes it would dive and they would have to guess where it would come up again. It seemed to be playing with them. It could stay under the water for a long time, but it never went too far before it surfaced again. Finally it disappeared. They all waited. Sam quivered with curiosity.

Karen said, "He's gone." Her face showed her disappointment.

"No, he's not. I can see him on shore. How did he get over there so quickly? Look, he's by those big rocks, just climbing that muddy bank. He must have his home around here. Let's follow him." Roger began to struggle with his oars now. The wind had really come up and rowing against the rippled water was becoming difficult. He forgot about the animal as he concentrated on his rowing. He tried to head closer to shore. He knew he must not let the boat drift into deeper water.

• When setting out, try to row against the wind or current to start with, so that it will be easier coming back.

14

Drop Anchor Here!

Do you remember when Karen and Roger had to change places? This is sometimes necessary when you are in a dinghy, but don't do it too often. A dinghy tips easily. Here's how you can prove it to yourself:

Balancing Act

Next time you are in the bath, take a large styrofoam meat tray and two equal weights, such as new blocks of soap.

Put the soap on the tray so that the tray does not tip over. Did you notice that the closer the two blocks are together, near the centre of the boat, the better balance you get? Now, change the position of the soaps so that the tray tips. Why did it tip? Did you put the two pieces too close to one end or too close to one side? There was nothing to balance that weight.

Now put the soaps back where they were, so that the tray balances. Move each one a bit at a time as if you were trying to change places in a boat. You will find the easiest—and safest—way is to move the soaps towards each other down the centre-line of the tray and then carefully around each other.

And this is the safest way to change places in a boat, if you must. Keep close together and maintain the balance!

Now, suppose you're in the boat by yourself? Well, you don't have another person to worry about, but you'll still find the boat is quite likely to tip up if you go too close to one side or the other. So always stay in the middle. If you are getting into an empty boat, make sure you step right into the middle of it.

Suppose you are in the boat by yourself and another person wants to get in? Try it with the soap again. Put one bar in the middle, where you would be sitting. Now place the other bar so that the tray doesn't tip. You'll find you have to put it quite close to the first bar, otherwise the tray will tip. This is what would happen to a boat if your passenger stepped in too close to the side or the end.

2: Rough Weather Ahead

"Sit down, Sam, you're going to tip us!" said Karen, as Sam began to shift his position to get a better view of the animal on the shore. The dinghy rocked crazily as he tried to pass Roger to get to the bow of the boat. "Sit, Sam!"

Roger heave-ho'd on the oars. The waves were getting higher. He knew that he ought to get closer to the shore as quickly as he could. By steadily pulling on the oars, he managed to prevent the wind from pushing the boat further away from the shore, but he couldn't get much closer in.

As he struggled he asked, "By the way, Karen, do you know what that animal is?"

"I suppose you think it's a mermaid," replied Karen, knowing how much he liked to daydream and probably was on a pirate adventure again.

"No! It's an otter. Have you ever seen a real one before? It looks just like the one in my book about animals. It sure can move beautifully in water, but did you see how clumsy it is on land?"

After a while, they realized that the wind direction was changing. It was easier now to row towards the shore. They entered a shallow bay almost totally surrounded by trees.

Karen was feeling a little shivery. Maybe it was just the change in the weather. "Don't you think that we should start trying to get back to the *Serendipity*?" she asked.

"We can't until this wind shifts direction again."

"I guess we'll just have to sit it out, then. We can't drag the dinghy over that rocky beach," Karen said. "At least we're safe here in this bay."

As they drifted around the bay, they peered up at the huge trees. Some near the water dripped long moss like witch's hair. The water was so shallow and clear that they could see all the way to the bottom. *I wonder if we will find any sunken treasure,* Roger fantasized. Little fish darted to and fro over the pebbly bottom. Roger noticed the otter gliding underwater like a submarine. Everything was quiet and still.

Then, "Woof! Woof!" Sam barked at something that only he could see on shore. Suddenly he dove overboard, and Karen and Roger hung on to the gunnels until the rocking ceased.

"Sam! Sam!" they shouted but Sam was almost ashore and had a bead on something more interesting. He scrambled out, shook himself thoroughly and disappeared into the trees. They could hear him barking and crashing through the undergrowth.

"Do you think there are bears here?" asked Roger. "Dad says that this looks like good bear country."

"Well, there might be, but I don't think right here," replied Karen in her pretending-not-to-be-scared voice. "And let's not worry about Sam. He can look after himself. At least if he's ashore he isn't rocking the boat. We can pick him up later when we go back to the *Serendipity*."

"'Why don't we go ashore, too, and tie up the boat?" asked Roger.

"The shoreline is too rough here. Besides, Dad says it's safer to stay with the boat when you are in unfamiliar territory."

It *was* a spooky sort of place, just ideal for a pirate to explore. Roger pulled first on one oar and then on the other. He'd noticed they sometimes did this in pirate movies. Then he decided to row standing up. He'd seen that in pirate movies, too. He spotted something.

"Look at that eagle, Karen. It has to be the biggest

one I've ever seen!"

As he pointed, he lost his balance.

"Oh, Roger! Sit down!" shouted Karen. But it was too late. The boat rocked wildly as Roger tumbled into the water, taking an oar with him.

• Take short strokes when rowing and don't dig the oars in too deep.

Drop Anchor Here!

Apart from Roger standing up in the boat—a thing you should never do—the children also got into a bit of trouble because the wind came up and the water got rough. A change in the weather is something to look out for. Ships' captains always make sure that they know just what's going on out there. They know that a certain kind of cloud formation or the wind blowing from a particular direction can be a warning of changing weather.

So, they keep a **ship's log.** It's often a good idea to keep a log even on a small boat because it ensures that you have taken the weather into account before you set off. Also, you can record other information such as whether an area is good for fishing or anchoring. Then you can look back on it when you are in that area again.

Here is Roger and Karen's log.

SHIP'S LOG FOR THE DINGHY . . . .

Date . . . .

Skipper . . . .

Destination . . . .

Place of departure . . . .

Weather . . . .

Wind force . . . .

Weather Watch

These are some signs to look for that tell you that the tide or weather are changing. Learn about a **barometer** and how to read a **compass.**

- Look at the sky. If the clouds get darker or thicker and blot out the sun, probably rain is coming.

- Look at any trees nearby. If they seem to be moving more than before, a storm may be on its way.

- Look at the water. If the surface seems ruffled or whitecaps can be seen in the distance, a storm is definitely on its way.

- Look at the shoreline if you are on the ocean. You can tell whether the tide is rising or falling depending on the amount of barnacles or seaweed you can see above the water line. Keep an eye on it, every fifteen minutes or so. Watch the level change.

Remember the saying: "Red sky at night, sailor's . delight; red sky in the morning, sailors take warning."

. . . .

Time of departure . . . .

Time of arrival:

      Estimated . . . .

      Actual . . . .

Wind direction . . . .

Tide . . . .

3: Man Overboard!

Roger bobbed up like a cork, barely touching the bottom before he surfaced again. He sputtered and thrashed in the water, not knowing quite where he was.

"It's okay, Roger. Just relax and let your lifejacket hold you up. I'll get you," Karen reassured him. She took the oar and stretched out to reach her brother. He grabbed it, almost pulling it out of her hands. She pulled him in closer until she could grab both his hands and put them on the side of the dinghy with hers firmly on top.

"Take it easy, Roger. Listen to me and do what I say." She echoed her mother's voice. "I'm going to lean on the side of the boat nearest you so you can get one arm and one leg over the gunnel, then I'll shift to the other side to balance the boat while you climb in."

Roger was too waterlogged to say anything. They had practised this many times before, diving from the dinghy and pulling themselves back in. But those times had just been a game, and Dad had always been there.

"Are you ready?" Karen asked. The boat tilted towards Roger as he got one leg in. Then he rested for a moment, exhausted by his efforts and by the cold water.

"Maybe we'd better tie this rope around your waist," said Karen. "Then I can pull on it and help you in." She passed the rope around his chest and secured it with a bowline.

"Okay," said Roger, now quite rested. With Karen's help he rolled over the gunnel and lay panting on the bottom of the boat like a beached whale.

"Are you all right?"

"Of course I'm all right," Roger replied. But he felt just like a pirate that had been keelhauled.

"Now," said practical Karen, "You get out of those wet things and wrap yourself in this blanket." She reached under the stern seat and took out the large plastic bag in which all the supplies were stored. She found the blanket and a rather big spare lifejacket.

"I'm not changing in front of you!" was Roger's indignant comment.

"Don't be silly!" his sister ordered. "You have to take off those wet clothes before you can get warm. Look, I'll turn and face the bow. Take off everything! Wrap yourself up and put this old lifejacket on top."

Roger did as he was told. He knew that she was right. He looked rather soggy and unhappy.

Karen took off her scarf. "Here, tie this around your head and then you'll look like a real pirate," she said as she reached for the remaining can of juice and Granola bar. She offered them to him. "If we want any more food after this, we'll have to pretend we're pirates and rob the *Serendipity*." Karen tried to humour him. "I think we should head back to Mom and Dad soon."

Roger, busy chewing an enormous mouthful, had nothing to say. The sky was really dark now. It sure was chilly! He shivered as he scanned the treetops, looking for the eagle that had caused all this trouble in the first place. Sam was sitting on the beach by now, having finished chasing imaginary rabbits.

"Are you finished?" asked Karen, anxious to start back to their parents' big, warm boat. Roger huddled in the bow while Karen settled herself on the centre thwart. Suddenly she cried, "Roger, we lost an oar when you fell in!"

"Look!" He pointed. "There it is, over by the shore! We're drifting that way, too. Maybe we can catch up to it!"

Karen tried to paddle with the remaining oar but the dinghy just kept going in circles. Roger reached a floating piece of driftwood and used it to balance her paddling. It took them a long time to go a short distance, and no matter how hard they tried, they

couldn't catch up with the drifting oar.

"I think we'll just have to wait until someone rescues us," said Roger.

"It'll be hours before someone comes," quavered Karen. "Mom and Dad are going to be worried. I wish we could send Sam all the way by land to get them."

Sam woofed when he heard his name. He didn't want to go in the water again but he would have liked to be back with his two friends. He hoped they wouldn't forget to pick him up when they left.

• Ship your oars (put them in the dinghy) when you are not using them. Tie your dinghy securely when you leave it.

Drop Anchor Here!

Did you notice that Karen and Roger knew what to do when Roger fell overboard? The important thing is, they didn't panic. Roger knew that his lifejacket would hold him up and Karen stretched out the oar to him when she realized that he was too far away. When they were getting him aboard, they made sure the boat stayed balanced just like the soaps in the meat tray.

If somebody falls in the water, this is how you get them out:

- Don't panic. You both have lifejackets on.

- Get the boat next to the person in the water.

- Get their hands on to the side of the boat.

- Make sure the boat stays balanced, and tell the person to get one leg over the side of the boat.

- Then tell them to roll in.

If the swimmer is heavier than the person in the boat, it might be a good idea to get a rope around the swimmer. If you are very close to shore, it might be easier to tow the swimmer in to shallow water and beach the boat. If the person is injured or unconscious, get them to the beach, and roll them onto their side to drain the water out of them. **If you've learned mouth-to-mouth resuscitation, do it!**

Now, Cover Up!

Do you know what hypothermia is? If you fall in the water and stay in for some time before you are rescued, you begin to lose heat from your body and get *very* cold. In winter your parents will tell you to wear a hat, gloves, boots and a coat so you are almost completely covered up. That's to keep in your body heat. Karen knew that wet clothing takes the heat from our bodies and that it was very important for Roger to keep warm. So she made him take off his wet things and wrap up in a blanket.

Try this experiment with an adult supervising:

Get two sausage rolls and heat them up in the oven. Take them out and wrap one with a tea towel. Leave them both for fifteen minutes. What do you think will happen? Although both sausage rolls were hot after they'd been in the oven, the unwrapped one cooled down much faster than the wrapped one, just like you would get cold in winter if you didn't wear a coat. So remember to wrap yourself up warmly if the weather is cold.

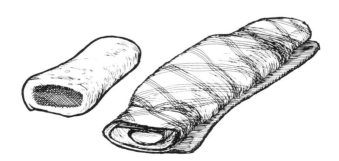

4: Drifting

Suddenly the sun popped from behind a cloud and they both felt a little better. Roger switched on his pirate role, feeling very much like a prisoner bound tightly in the blanket. The boat drifted on. Sam kept pace with them, moving along the shore. The eagle sat high in a bare tree, absolutely still. *He's the lookout,* Roger thought.

Just then, Roger remembered the walkie-talkie. "Let's call Mom and Dad!"

"Why didn't we think of that before?" Karen said. She shipped her oar and reached once more into the plastic bag, found the walkie-talkie and gave it to her brother.

Roger switched it on and adjusted the antenna. "Baby Bear to Papa Bear. Do you hear me? This is Baby Bear. Please answer." Roger looked at the shoreline which curved to hide the *Serendipity* from view. They had drifted a long way. Probably no one could hear them.

******

Over an hour had passed since the children had left the *Serendipity*. Mom decided to call them on the CB, hoping they had their walkie-talkie on. "Momma Bear to Baby Bear. Momma Bear to Goldilocks. Do you read me? Come in, please. . . . Bill, I can't raise them," she said to Dad. "Will you try?"

He couldn't get any reply either. "They must be out of range. Where could they have got to?"

"Oh, I hope they didn't go too far," said Mom worriedly.

"They can't be far away." He spread the chart and traced the area with his finger. "I don't think they could

have rowed very far—but the wind's got up since they left and they might have had difficulty rowing against it. I'm going to talk with the other boaters over there."

Since the children had the dinghy, Dad called to the nearest boater, who rowed over and picked him up. He rowed around to all the other boaters asking if they had seen two children and a large golden dog in a dinghy. Nobody had.

******

Meanwhile Karen was trying to paddle again. She wasn't *really* scared because they were close to land and anyway, Mom and Dad would come looking for them soon.

Roger, beginning to warm up a little from the sun and the warm blanket, announced, "I want to be put ashore with Sam."

"No, you have to stay here. You can't walk barefooted and wrapped up like a sausage."

Roger thought his pirate thoughts again. *Always giving orders! Next she'll make me walk the plank.* "I'm hungry and thirsty," he said aloud.

"What, again? You had the last of our snacks." She reached for the First Aid Kit. "I just remembered the candies Mom put in here. If we suck them, we won't be so thirsty." She unwrapped two, giving her brother his favorite grape flavour. Then she dug into the bag to see what else was in there. She found a flashlight and an airhorn, a whistle and a reflector. The reflector wouldn't be much good since there was nobody to flash it at, but the airhorn and the whistle would make lots of noise.

Karen also found some extra line stashed under the seat, and a baling can. She handed the can to Roger. "Here, empty some of the water out of the bottom of the boat."

"Do this! Do that," he muttered. *Bale out the water. Swab the decks,* he thought to himself. *She's just like Captain Bligh.* He scooped out a few cansful and then

absentmindedly slowed down as he watched a kingfisher diving for its dinner. He was really hungry. *You always starve on a pirate ship.* "Can I have another candy? A cherry one this time."

While Karen unwrapped another candy, Roger began to tap on the baling can, like a drum. *Maybe he could send a secret code to his pirate friends and they would come and rescue him from the clutches of this enemy captain.* "Tap-tap-tap, tap . . . tap . . . tap . . . tap-tap-tap!" he repeated over and over. "Hey, I remember! This is the SOS signal we learned at Cubs." Louder he tapped, "Tap-tap-tap, tap . . . tap . . . tap . . . tap-tap-tap!"

"Great!" said Karen. "Keep it up. The more noise we make, the more likely someone will find us. I'm going to use this small orange plastic bag to make a float. It will help the rescuers to see us." She busied herself blowing air into it and then twisted and tied the top into a knot so the air would not escape. It looked like a huge balloon. She fastened it so it would float near the dinghy.

• Be careful beaching the boat; you do not want to damage the bottom.

Drop Anchor Here!

Well, it looks as though Karen and Roger won't be found right away. But they really aren't in any trouble. They will be seen because they are wearing bright life jackets and Karen has made an orange float. They know they have to try to attract attention by signalling or making a noise. Although the children don't know it, *we* know that their parents are already trying to find them.

Morse Code

Here's a way you can make sure you are seen or heard. The Morse Code is used for signalling at sea. It consists of dots and dashes and can be signalled by a flashlight or by tapping, as Roger did.

A ._	H	N _.	T _
B _...	I ..	O _ _ _	U .._
C _._.	J ._ _ _	P ._ _.	V ..._
D _..	K _._	Q _ _._	W ._ _
E .	L ._..	R ._.	X _.._
F .._.	M _ _	S ...	Y _._ _
G _ _.			Z _ _..

Here, once more, is the SOS that Roger used. You can use a flashlight to flash a signal using the letters for SOS or you can tap them out as Roger did with the can.

SOS = ..._ _ _...

Bright Colours are Best

Here's an experiment you can do to show how bright colours show up so that you can be seen.

Find a large coloured picture of an outdoor scene. Cut two small holes in the picture. Tape some orange paper behind one hole and some blue paper behind the other. Stand back and look at the picture from a distance. Which colour stands out the best? The orange, of course, because orange is a bright colour which you don't often find in nature. Try this experiment on someone else and see if they agree.

Dinghy Equipment Checklist

The equipment on Roger and Karen's dinghy was kept dry in a plastic bag so that it was in good shape when they needed it. Here are some things that you must have on board a dinghy before you set off:

- 2 oars and oarlocks
- lifejacket for each person aboard
- 1 baling can
- 1 blanket
- 1 bowline and 1 sternline
- 1 First Aid Kit
- 1 flashlight
- 1 whistle (be sure it will work when damp)
- 1 reflector (a small mirror or shiny lid)
- 2 large garbage bags (for raincoats or shelter)
- 1 small orange garbage bag (to make a float)

5: Bags Have Many Uses

While Karen and Roger were making sure that they could be seen and heard by any rescuers in the area, Dad had got together a few volunteers to help in the search.

"Well, Ann, we've got lots of help. Get on the CB and the VHF and try to make contact with anyone in the area. Give them a description of the dinghy, the kids and the dog."

Mom raised several boaters and even a trucker on shore, but no one had seen the children.

She tried to contact the walkie-talkie again. "Baby Bear! Baby Bear! This is Momma Bear. Do you hear me? Come in, please, Baby Bear! Do you hear me, Goldilocks?" She repeated the message several times but the children didn't answer. "I guess they can't hear me," she said to Dad.

"I'm sure they're okay," said Dad. "They're pretty smart kids and they've been boating all their lives. They know enough to stay put if they are in trouble. Now, you stay here and keep the CB turned on in case they try to call. I'll take the other walkie-talkie with me. Every boat around here has either a CB or a VHF on. We'll find them."

Four boats headed out to search for the children.

******

Karen made sure that her orange marker was fastened to the dinghy and floating on the side facing the open water. Then she relaxed a little, feeling that they had done all that they could for now. She felt a little chilly

and, once more, looked around her at the trees, now moving about in the breeze. It was definitely getting cloudier. The water looked quite rough beyond the bay.

"Roger, stop tapping for a while. I need your help to rig up some kind of shelter. It sure looks like rain and it's starting to get dark." A big black cloud sat right over them. The kingfisher kept fishing and the eagle kept sitting in his tree, and Sam.... Where was Sam? Karen couldn't see him anywhere. "Sam! Sam! Where are you? Sam! Come back!" she called.

"He can't be far. I saw him just a few minutes ago, heading along the shore," said Roger.

"That's all right, then. Now, you untie the knots in this line while I rip up one side of this spare plastic bag. We can make it into a tent!" Then she used a piece of driftwood like a tent pole, propping up the bag while Roger tied the corners to the gunnels.

"There should be room for both of us under here," she said, when they had finished.

"I'm going to hoist a pirate flag on top, too," said Roger, using the scarf Karen had loaned him and hoping that his pirate mates would see it.

They finished just in time. Huge raindrops began to bounce off the surface of the water. They huddled under their shelter. It kept their heads dry, though Karen's bare legs were very cold. She put up her hood and zipped her jacket right to the top, readjusted her lifejacket and tucked her feet under Roger. Roger was nice and snug in his warm blanket which covered him from head to toe. *When will Dad and Mom come?* they both wondered.

Roger kept the walkie-talkie in one hand, every so often trying to transmit a message. With the other hand he baled the water from the bottom of the boat which seemed to be accumulating quite quickly now, with the heavy rain.

Karen occasionally used the one oar to try to keep them as close to shore as possible. Luckily the wind had died down when it started raining.

******

44

After half an hour, the search boats returned to the anchorage for a discussion. Nobody had seen the children.

"I think the wind must have blown them quite a long way," said Dad. "When the wind roughs up the water, it can move a boat along at a good clip and a child would have a hard time rowing against it. I hope they're near this shore and haven't drifted out into open water. Let's do one more search. Then we'd better call in some outside help, like Search and Rescue. It's starting to get dark."

• Always turn the bow of the boat into big waves.

Drop Anchor Here!

Like all sailors, Karen and Roger found that there were times when they needed to know how to tie knots which were easy to untie, yet would not come undone accidentally. Sailors use many knots and it's difficult to remember them all. Luckily there are only three that are really important for younger boaters.

- The Round Turn and Two Half Hitches, which you would use for tying the boat to a tree, a ring or a bollard.

- The Bowline, for tying a loop in the end of a line, like Karen did when she tied the rope around Roger.

- The Reef Knot, for tying two ends of a rope together after you've put it round something.

But first, we want to find out how to use a cleat. A cleat is a metal or wood fitting with two projecting ends. Wrap the line once around the base of the cleat, then lead it over the top of the cleat and under one projection, to form a figure eight. Make one more figure eight and *finish with an underhand loop,* so that the line is pulled tight against itself. If you do this properly, it won't work loose when the boat rocks about.

The main knots are easy to remember if you invent little stories to describe how they are tied, like this:

Round Turn and Two Half Hitches

The flying ace zooms past the airport, banks and does another circuit, then loops the loop twice.

Reef knot

The baby elephant steps over the log, under the bridge and over the crocodile, hears his mother call and goes back over the crocodile, under the bridge and over the log.

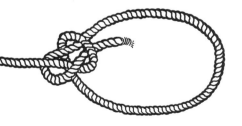

Bowline

The scared rabbit pops out of his hole, round the tree and down his hole again.

6: Rescued!

Evening closed in on the children.

"Hey," said Roger, "do you think we could lasso that tree? Paddle us a little closer in to shore and I'll try to grab it as we drift by." He slipped into his pirate role once again as he prepared to board the enemy vessel. *A toss of the rope and he had it looped around the railing of the pirate ship.* Quickly he fastened it with a couple of hitches. *They were ready to board.*

"Good," said Karen, bringing him out of his daydream. "Now we'll stay put till Dad and Mom come."

Roger looked at his hand. "I've got a sliver," he said.

"Let me see. . . . I think I can pull it out."

"I don't want you to touch it. It hurts!"

"Come on. It won't hurt so much after we get it out. You hold the flashlight steady for me."

"Okay, but give me another grape candy."

"Hold out your hand." She closed the tweezers on the sliver and pulled it gently out. Then she smeared some First Aid cream on the place and covered it with a bandaid. "All finished," she said.

Roger had been gritting his teeth and holding his breath, pretending his surgery was being performed by a pirate mate using a dagger, heated in a flame for sterilization. He was almost disappointed that it was all over so fast. He'd been feeling so brave. He always felt much braver in his world of make-believe. But now, in the real world, it was getting dark and he was just a bit scared.

Karen was shivering from the cold. "Here, share part of the blanket," said Roger.

"Thanks," Karen poked her head out of the tent and called, "Sam! Where are you? Sam! Come here!"

But Sam was nowhere around. They couldn't even hear him crashing through the bush. It was cold and wet and dark and they were alone.

******

Meanwhile, Dad and the other boaters were making one last search, following each bay and point along the shoreline with their spotlights.

"Karen! Roger!" they shouted.

Dad used his walkie-talkie to keep in touch with the *Serendipity*. "We're going a little further along the shore. Then we'll head back and I'll give you the details for Search and Rescue. Hang in there, Ann. We'll find them!"

The rescuers continued to play their high-powered spotlights on the shore. "What's that shining over there?" someone shouted.

"Where?"

"There! It looks like a pair of eyes."

"Woof! Woof!"

"Sam! That's Sam! I'd know that bark anywhere!" shouted Dad. "Sam! Where are Karen and Roger?"

As if knowing exactly what was being said to him, Sam barked again and bounded away.

Where's he going? Dad wondered.

Suddenly a metallic voice came from the walkie-talkie, "Goldilocks to Momma Bear. Goldilocks to Papa Bear. Do you read me?"

"It's Karen!" shouted Dad. "Papa Bear to Goldilocks. I read you. Come in, Goldilocks!"

"Daddy, I think I can see your lights further along the shore. Is that you, Daddy?"

"Yes, Karen, it's me. Is Roger okay?"

"He's fine but we've lost Sam."

"We saw him. I think he's heading your way. Are you on shore, too?"

"No, not exactly. We're tied up to a tree. We thought you'd never come. Can you see our light now? Roger

has been flashing an SOS for a long time."

"We can see you. Just shine a steady beam. Sam will lead us right to you."

"There they are!" shouted everyone at once.

"Woof, woof!" barked Sam.

"Daddy!" shouted the children.

******

Safely back on the *Serendipity*, the children were snuggled in their warm sleeping bags with steaming cups of hot chocolate.

"How long were we gone?" asked Karen.

"It was about three hours," replied Mom.

"It seemed much longer, didn't it, Roger?"

Roger didn't hear. *He was fast asleep in his hammock, dreaming his pirate adventure.*

"All I can say," said Dad, "is that you children may have made a few mistakes at first, but after that you really did all the right things. You should feel really good about yourselves. Your Mom and I are proud of you."

"Woof," said Sam.

"You were great, too, Sam."

Drop Anchor Here!

Back on board, safe at last! These two children should be proud of themselves. They aren't very old but they have picked up lots of information about boating and safety afloat. Will *you* be so well prepared when you next take out a dinghy on your own?

There is one more thing you should do before taking out your dinghy: check your First Aid Box. Of course, you should know a little bit about treating a patient. The best thing to do is to take a First Aid course.

If an accident happens:

- Make the injured person feel safe by letting them know that you are there and that help is coming.

- If the person seems badly wounded, don't move them, just cover them to keep them warm.

- If the person is bleeding heavily, take the cleanest material you can find and press it hard against the wound.

- If the wound has a small sliver that seems easy to pull out, take it out but if there is something larger, like glass or any other sharp object, leave it alone till someone experienced comes.

- If it's a small wound, use a little disinfectant and cover it with a bandaid.

Your First Aid Kit

These are the basic supplies you should have in your First Aid Kit:

- bandaids
- disinfectant or cream
- tweezers
- a pressure bandage
- larger pads for larger wounds
- gauze bandage
- hard, wrapped candies
- a pair of scissors

Well, it looks as though you might be ready to be awarded a Dinghy Operator's Licence. If you have practiced all these things, find someone to test you.

Safety Afloat

Karen and Roger came through this experience with flying colours. There was really only one unsafe act in the whole episode: Roger, lost in his imagination, was *standing up to row*. Otherwise, the two children confidently displayed their knowledge of water safety and rescue procedures. They were aware of the force of the wind, the need for protection from the cold, methods of signalling, simple First Aid and, above all, that they should stay with the boat in the area where their parents would expect them to be. Of course, they were a little apprehensive at times, but generally they were confident that their parents would find them.

Perhaps the parents had become over-confident in their children's ability. They set no limits on distance or time. They should have established a time when all would monitor their walkie-talkies, just to keep in touch. Obviously, children in a dinghy could not be far away, but currents, winds and tides can be very unpredictable. Nevertheless the children kept calm, treating what could have been a serious incident as an adventure. The parents had trained them well.

Karen and Roger were confident and resourceful because their parents had encouraged safety consciousness, awareness of hazards and, above all, lots of practice.

Parents — Prepare that Child!

Although this adventure is fiction, all of these incidents *could* happen. Karen and Roger were part of a boating family that had spent time learning together, discussing the dangers, allaying the fears. The family had equipped both their *Serendipity* and their dinghy well.

If you are seasoned boaters, this tale and accompanying activities will remind you that checking equipment and practising skills should be routine. No one would fly a plane without observing certain safety procedures and routine maintenance, yet so many boaters fail to take that little bit of extra time before leaving the dock.

If you are new to boating, be sure that your children learn *with* you. Your life may be in their hands. Anyone can fall overboard or be hurt and unable to perform necessary jobs. Besides, children who are made to feel they are part of the crew enjoy boating more.

There are six main areas that should be stressed when teaching a child to be self-reliant afloat:

- **Be responsible aboard:** wear a lifejacket at all times, change places carefully and ship oars when they are not in use.

- **Be aware of the elemental hazards of your boating area:** wind, current, tides and shoreline.

- **Be knowledgeable of safety procedures in the water:** how to rescue yourself or someone else and how to protect against hypothermia.

- **Be calm when in distress:** be confident that help is available if you help yourself, make yourself visible, protect yourself from the elements and communicate by making a noise or signalling.

- **Be able to tie basic knots and know the best use of each one.**

- **Be able to carry out simple First Aid.**

Some skills are best taught by boating parents and adapted to your family's needs. Not all dinghies handle alike. Your local boating area will have its own characteristics; children should be encouraged to explore and read about it. Landmarks should be recognized and the use of a compass should be routine. Use of equipment such as walkie-talkies, a CB or the VHF should be explained and practiced. If there were an emergency, you might be glad your child could operate them.

Other skills can be learned at school, Scouts and Guides, Boys and Girls clubs, the Y, swimming pools and junior boating clubs. Learning to swim should be the first priority. Simple First Aid and prevention of hypothermia should be taught. Many organizations have good programs of interest to boating children.

Here are some additional ideas:

- **Rowing practice.** Even a small child of three or four, dressed in an approved lifejacket, can learn to row. Tie one end of a long line to the stern of your boat and the other to the stern of the dinghy. Let the child row. It is easy to haul in on the line if the child becomes tired or discouraged.

- **Dinghy procedures.** Allow a child to practice docking and beaching the dinghy. Encourage tying lines to cleats, rings, trees and around rocks.

Children soon learn for themselves how hard it is to row ashore against a current, or to dock when the wind is blowing against them.

• **Man Overboard practice.** While in lifejackets and tied as for rowing practice, play 'Man Overboard'. One jumps in, the other assists in the 'rescue'. As an adult, take part in the game, be the 'Man Overboard' and let the children find out how hard it is to rescue a larger person. This game is fine until they become cold. At this point, they should be made aware of the effects of hypothermia and should dry off and change.

• **Resuscitation.** Understand and practice the correct techniques.

• **Walkie-talkies.** Children should be taught the correct procedures for using walkie-talkies. They should experiment to find out the range, observe that others can communicate on the same frequency and that they can pick up CB signals. Later they will understand how to operate CB's and VHF's.

• **Morse Code and the International Alphabet.** These are most useful when boating. It's fun for a child to learn them and play games with them. The International Alphabet is one of the criteria for a Radio Licence.

• **Dinghy and First Aid supplies.** Since the dinghy is often used by children, give them the responsibility of checking the equipment aboard as if they were in a cockpit of a plane before takeoff.

Help your children to enjoy boating by learning and participating. You, the parents, set the standards.

Colleen and Joan's Letter

Dear Parents:

When teaching children, it is most important to build on what they know and to encourage them to develop self-confidence. Many people are afraid of the water. If children are exposed to water by a natural progression from bathtub to backyard pool, to swimming pool, to ocean, they will soon feel confident in their ability to deal with it. Roger and Karen respected the possibility of danger but never showed fear of the water, even when Roger fell in. They did become a little anxious when the realized they had been gone for some time and that it was getting dark. However, they never panicked. They believed that their parents would come and, in the meantime, they kept busy.

We can help children to deal with crises in three ways: *discussing* the possibilities of what could happen and encouraging imaginative solving of hypothetical problems; providing opportunities for *practice* and *experimentation* within a safe environment; and allowing them to "take command" of situations so that they *experience* being in control and having others depend on them.

It is our hope that your boating will always be enjoyable and accident-free and that this book will help to ensure your children's safety afloat.

Happy boating,

Colleen & Joan

Dinghy Operator's Licence

Haning met the conditions required,

_____

is awarded this licence to operate the dinghy,

_____

Signed _____

Dated_____

This licence must be renewed each boating season.

Having met the following conditions, the person named on the face of this certificate is now qualified to be licenced as a Dinghy Operator.

- Must always wear a lifejacket.

- Must be able to swim.

- Must be able to board, row, ship oars and disembark from a dinghy without adult assistance.

- Must have learned about local water and weather conditions and be able to complete a log.

- Must have practiced and mastered 'Man Overboard' drills.

- Must understand hypothermia and what to do to help prevent it.

- Must be able to tie the three basic knots and know their uses, and be able to fasten a line securely to a cleat.

- Must know simple First Aid and be able to list the basic contents of a First Aid kit.

- Must have practiced methods of communication: SOS, walkie-talkie, arm signals, etc.